# ULTIMATE RED VELVET VANILLA AND CHOCOLATE RECIPE

*"Indulge in Sweet Harmony: Unleashing the Delectable Secrets of Ultimate Red Velvet, Vanilla, and Chocolate Recipes"*

# COPYRIGHT

# Table of Contents

# ABOUT AUTHOR

My name is Oyeronke Shittu, my bakery name is sugarinstinctcakes, I am a self-taught home baker, recipe developer. I am passionate about sharing all my recipes that are filled with tips and tricks and are easy to follow so you can enjoy an amazing cake in the comfort of your home.

I had always been a fan of baking, but it wasn't until I moved out on my own that I really began to experiment in the kitchen. I started small, with simple recipes like chocolate chip cookies and brownies. But as I gained confidence in my baking abilities, I started to venture out and try more complex recipes.

One day, I came across a recipe for a chocolate cake that looked absolutely divine. I had all of the ingredients on hand, so I decided to give it a try.

The process of making the cake was a bit more involved than I was used to, but I followed the recipe closely and was careful to measure everything accurately. As I mixed and stirred the batter, I could already tell that this was going to be a delicious cake.

When it was finally time to put the cake in the oven, I was a bit nervous. I had never made a cake before, and I wasn't sure if it was going to turn out as I had hoped. But I took a deep breath and placed the cake pan in the oven, crossing my fingers for good luck.

As the minutes ticked by, the aroma of the baking cake began to fill my kitchen. It was a tantalizing blend of chocolate and sugar, and I could hardly wait for it to be done.

Finally, after what seemed like an eternity, the timer went off and I pulled the cake out of the oven. It looked absolutely perfect, with a rich, dark chocolate color and a moist, fluffy texture.

I couldn't wait to dig in, but I knew I had to let the cake cool first. So I set it aside and tried to distract myself with other tasks while I waited.

When the cake was finally cool enough to slice, I couldn't resist the temptation any longer. I carefully cut myself a slice, savoring the rich chocolate flavor and the soft, tender crumb. It was one of the best cakes I had ever tasted, and I knew I had to share it with my friends and family.

Over the next few weeks, I baked that chocolate cake again and again, perfecting the recipe each time. I started to experiment with different variations, adding different flavors and frostings to the mix. And before I knew it, I had developed a whole collection of delicious cake recipes that I loved to share with others.

Baking had always been a hobby for me, but as I discovered my passion for creating delicious, beautiful cakes, it became so much more. It became a way for me to express myself, to share my love of food with others, and to bring a little bit of joy into the world. And I knew that, no matter where my journey took me, I would always have a special place in my heart for the humble cake slice. So lets get baking!

# VANILLA CAKE

I absolutely love vanilla cakes! They have been my favorite dessert for as long as I can remember. I think my love for vanilla cake stems from my childhood and the memories associated with it.

Whenever there was a special occasion in my family, such as a birthday or a holiday, my mother would always bake a delicious vanilla cake. I remember the sweet aroma that would fill the house as it baked in the oven, and the excitement I felt as I waited for it to cool down so that I could have a slice. Those moments were always filled with joy and happiness, and I think that is why I associate vanilla cake with familial themes.

As a child, vanilla cake was also my go-to dessert when I needed comfort. It was something that I knew would always make me feel better, no matter what was going on in my life. I would often come home from school feeling stressed or upset, and my mother would have a freshly baked vanilla cake waiting for me. Eating a slice of that cake would instantly make me feel better and remind me that everything was going to be okay.

Now as an adult, whenever I have a slice of vanilla cake, it takes me back to those childhood memories and the comfort and happiness that it brought me. It's not just a dessert for me, it's a symbol of love, family, and comfort. That's why I will always love vanilla cakes, and they will always hold a special place in my heart.

Vanilla cake is a light, fluffy cake made with flour, sugar, eggs, butter, milk, and vanilla extract or vanilla essence. It is a simple and classic cake flavor that is widely enjoyed and is often used as a base for various frostings, fillings, and toppings. This cake is so delicious and soft, they are also very easy to make.

Vanilla cake is loved for several reasons, including:

- Simplicity: Vanilla cake is a classic flavor that is simple and unassuming. It doesn't have any overpowering flavors, making it a safe choice for people who are not fond of strong or unusual tastes.

- Versatility: Vanilla cake is versatile and can be paired with a wide range of flavors and toppings, such as fresh fruit, chocolate, whipped cream, or buttercream frosting. This allows for a wide range of customization and personalization, making it an ideal choice for various occasions and preferences.

- Comfort food: Vanilla cake can evoke a sense of nostalgia and comfort, as it is often associated with childhood memories, family gatherings, and celebrations. This emotional connection to the cake can make it a favorite among many people.

- Universality: Vanilla cake is also a flavor that is widely recognized and enjoyed across different cultures and regions. This universality makes it a go-to choice for many people, especially when trying to accommodate different tastes and preferences.

Overall, the simplicity, versatility, comfort, and universality of vanilla cake are some of the reasons why it is loved by all and sundry.

For a classic vanilla cake, some popular frosting options include:
1. Buttercream
2. Whipped Cream
3. Cream Cheese
4. Dark chocolate Ganache
5. White chocolate ganache

MY SIGNATURE VANILLA CAKE RECIPE:

## INGREDIENTS INCLUDE:

- Flour – 210grams
- Baking Powder – 6grams (1 &1/2tsp)
- Baking Soda – 3grams (1/2tsp)
- Salt - 3grams (1/2tsp)
- Fine Granulated Sugar: 210grams
- Unsalted Butter Softened: 70grams
- Vegetable Oil – 60ml
- Greek. Yoghurt or Sour Cream: 85grams
- Pure Vanilla Extract: 5ml (1tsp)
- Whole Milk: 200ml

## METHOD

1. Preheat oven to 350F (180C). Grease two 6- inch pans with the cake release.

2. Sift flour, baking powder, baking soda and salt into the bowl of your stand mixer. Add in the granulated sugar.

3. In the bowl of your food processor or blender, add in Greek yogurt.

4. Followed by softened butter.

5. Add unflavored oil

6. Add eggs.

7. Add vanilla flavor. Emulsify and set aside.

8. Heat the milk in the microwave for 45 seconds, or until it reaches a temperature between 140-158F OR 60-70c. You don't need to bring it to a boil.

9. Add all wet ingredients in the food processor or blender and emulsify into a liquid form.

10. Using a handheld or stand mixer fitted with a paddle attachment, stir the dry ingredients on the lowest speed for 1 minute.

11. Add the wet ingredients from your blender and mix on medium speed until combined. DO NOT OVERMIX.

12. Slowly add in the hot milk, and mix for 1 minute till combined.

13.Sieve the batter to achieve a smooth consistency.

14. Divide the batter into two small 6 inches pan, you can also weigh them for accuracy.

15. Bake for 30-40 minutes or until a wooden skewer inserted into the middle of the cake comes out clean.

16. Remove the cake from the oven and allow to cool down completely the pans set on the wire rack.

17.Cover cakes and wrap using a plastic wrap to seal in moisture, and chill in the refrigerator till you are ready to decorate or eat.

OTHER VANILLA RECIPES YOU CAN TRY OUT:

### 1. Basic Vanilla Cake

- 2 cups all-purpose flour
- 1 1/2 cups granulated sugar
- 2 teaspoons baking powder
- 1/2 teaspoon salt
- 1/2 cup unsalted butter, at room temperature
- 2 large eggs
- 1 cup whole milk
- 1 teaspoon vanilla extract

## Instructions:

Preheat the oven to 350°F. In a bowl, mix together flour, sugar, baking powder, and salt. In another bowl, beat butter until creamy. Add eggs one at a time, beating well after each addition. Mix in milk and vanilla. Gradually add dry ingredients to the wet mixture, beating until just combined. Pour batter into a greased 9-inch cake pan and bake for 30-35 minutes or until a toothpick inserted comes out clean.

## 2. Classic Vanilla Sponge Cake

- 1 1/2 cups all-purpose flour
- 1 teaspoon baking powder
- 1/2 teaspoon salt
- 1/2 cup unsalted butter, at room temperature
- 1 cup granulated sugar
- 2 large eggs
- 1/2 cup whole milk
- 1 teaspoon vanilla extract

## Instructions:

Preheat oven to 350°F. In a bowl, sift together flour, baking powder, and salt. In another bowl, cream butter and sugar until fluffy. Add eggs one at a time, beating well after each addition. Mix in milk and vanilla. Gradually add dry ingredients to the wet mixture, beating until just combined. Pour batter into a greased 9-inch cake pan and bake for 30-35 minutes or until a toothpick inserted comes out clean.

## 1. Vanilla Pound Cake

- 2 cups all-purpose flour
- 1/2 teaspoon baking powder

- 1/2 teaspoon salt
- 1 cup unsalted butter, at room temperature
- 2 cups granulated sugar
- 4 large eggs
- 1/2 cup whole milk
- 1 teaspoon vanilla extract

## Instructions:

Preheat oven to 325°F. In a bowl, mix together flour, baking powder, and salt. In another bowl, cream butter and sugar until fluffy. Add eggs one at a time, beating well after each addition. Mix in milk and vanilla. Gradually add dry ingredients to the wet mixture, beating until just combined. Pour batter into a greased 9-inch cake pan and bake for 60-70 minutes or until a toothpick inserted comes out clean.

3. **Vanilla Layer Cake**
- 3 cups all-purpose flour
- 1 tablespoon baking powder
- 1/2 teaspoon salt
- 1 cup unsalted butter, at room temperature
- 2 cups granulated sugar
- 4 large eggs

- 1 cup whole milk
- 1 tablespoon vanilla extract

## Instructions:

Preheat oven to 350°F. In a bowl, mix together flour, baking powder, and salt. In another bowl, cream butter and sugar until fluffy. Add eggs one at a time, beating well after each addition. Mix in milk and vanilla. Gradually add dry ingredients to the wet mixture, beating until just combined. Divide batter evenly between 3 greased 9-inch cake pans and bake for 20-25 minutes or until a toothpick inserted comes out clean.

### 4. Vanilla Cupcakes

- 1 1/2 cups all-purpose flour
- 1 teaspoon baking powder
- 1/2 teaspoon salt
- 1/2 cup unsalted butter, at room temperature
- 1 cup granulated sugar
- 2 large eggs
- 1/2Cup whole milk
- 1 teaspoon vanilla extract

## Instructions:

Preheat oven to 350°F. In a bowl, mix together flour, baking powder, and salt. In another bowl, cream butter and sugar until fluffy. Add eggs one at a time, beating well after each addition. Mix in milk and vanilla. Gradually add dry ingredients to the wet mixture, beating until just combined. Line a cupcake pan with cupcake liners and fill each cupcake liner 2/3 full with batter. Bake for 18-20 minutes or until a toothpick inserted comes out clean.

### 5. Vanilla Chiffon Cake

- 2 1/4 cups all-purpose flour
- 1 1/2 cups granulated sugar
- 1 tablespoon baking powder
- 1 teaspoon salt
- 1/2 cup vegetable oil
- 7 large eggs, separated
- 3/4 cup cold water
- 2 teaspoons vanilla extract

## Instructions:

Preheat oven to 325°F. In a bowl, sift together flour, sugar, baking powder, and salt. In another bowl, mix oil, egg yolks, water, and vanilla until well combined. Gradually add dry ingredients to the wet mixture, beating until just combined. In a separate bowl, beat egg whites until stiff peaks form. Fold egg whites into the batter until just combined. Pour batter into an ungreased 10-inch tube pan and bake for 55-60 minutes or until a toothpick inserted comes out clean.

### 6. Vanilla Sheet Cake

- 2 1/4 cups all-purpose flour
- 1 1/2 cups granulated sugar
- 1 tablespoon baking powder
- 1 teaspoon salt
- 1/2 cup unsalted butter, at room temperature
- 1 cup whole milk
- 2 large eggs
- 1 teaspoon vanilla extract

**Instructions:**

Preheat oven to 350°F. In a bowl, mix together flour, sugar, baking powder, and salt. In another bowl, cream butter until fluffy. Add eggs one at a time, beating well after each addition. Mix in milk and vanilla. Gradually add dry ingredients to the wet mixture, beating until just combined. Pour batter into a greased 13x9-inch baking pan and bake for 30-35 minutes or until a toothpick inserted comes out clean.

### 7. Vanilla Bundt Cake

- 3 cups all-purpose flour
- 1 tablespoon baking powder
- 1/2 teaspoon salt
- 1 1/2 cups unsalted butter, at room temperature
- 2 cups granulated sugar
- 6 large eggs
- 1 cup whole milk
- 2 teaspoons vanilla extract

## Instructions:

Preheat oven to 350°F. In a bowl, mix together flour, baking powder, and salt. In another bowl, cream butter and sugar until fluffy. Add eggs one at a time, beating well after each addition. Mix in milk and vanilla. Gradually add dry ingredients to the wet mixture, beating until just combined. Pour batter into a greased 10-cup bundt cake pan and bake for 60-70 minutes or until a toothpick inserted comes out clean.

## 8. Vanilla Buttermilk Cake

- 2 cups all-purpose flour
- 1 1/2 teaspoons baking powder
- 1/2 teaspoon baking soda
- 1/2 teaspoon salt
- 1/2 cup unsalted butter, at room temperature
- 1 1/4 cups granulated sugar
- 2 large eggs
- 1 teaspoon vanilla extract
- 1 cup buttermilk

## Instructions:

Preheat oven to 350°F. In a bowl, mix together flour, baking powder, baking soda, and salt. In another bowl, cream butter and sugar until fluffy. Add eggs one at a time, beating well after each addition. Mix in vanilla. Gradually add dry ingredients to the wet mixture, alternating with buttermilk, starting and ending with the dry ingredients. Mix until just combined. Pour batter into a greased 9-

inch cake pan and bake for 30-35 minutes or until a toothpick inserted comes out clean.

### 9. Vanilla Pound Cake

- 3 cups all-purpose flour
- 1 teaspoon baking powder
- 1/2 teaspoon baking soda
- 1/2 teaspoon salt
- 1 1/2 cups unsalted butter, at room temperature
- 2 cups granulated sugar
- 6 large eggs
- 1 teaspoon vanilla extract
- 1/2 cup whole milk

## Instructions:

Preheat oven to 350°F. In a bowl, mix together flour, baking powder, baking soda, and salt. In another bowl, cream butter and sugar until fluffy. Add eggs one at a time, beating well after each addition. Mix in vanilla. Gradually add dry ingredients to the wet mixture, alternating with milk, starting and ending with the dry ingredients. Mix until just combined. Pour batter into a greased 10-inch loaf pan and bake for 60-70 minutes or until a toothpick inserted comes out clean.

Note: These recipes are for vanilla cakes only. Feel free to add frosting or other toppings as desired.

# RED VELVET CAKE

I'll take you on a delightful journey through my first encounter with red velvet cake and how it ignited my passion for baking and selling this heavenly treat.

It was a bright summer morning when I embarked on a long-awaited vacation to the enchanting city of London. I had heard tales of its vibrant culture and mouthwatering delicacies, but little did I know that my life was about to change forever. As I strolled along the charming streets, a captivating aroma beckoned me towards a quaint little bakery nestled in a corner.

Stepping inside, I was instantly captivated by the warm ambiance and the delightful display of desserts. My eyes were immediately drawn to a velvety crimson cake sitting gracefully on a porcelain pedestal. I had heard whispers of its magic, but I had never tasted a red velvet cake before.

I approached the counter, my heart pounding with anticipation, and ordered a generous slice of the crimson masterpiece. The baker, with a twinkle in her eyes, handed me the slice with a gentle smile. Holding the fork in my trembling hand, I delicately brought the first bite to my lips.

As the fork sank into the moist layers, my taste buds were engulfed in a symphony of flavors. The cocoa infused with a subtle hint of vanilla danced upon my tongue, perfectly complemented by the velvety cream cheese frosting. It was a harmonious blend of sweetness and tanginess that left me utterly enchanted.

With every subsequent bite, I felt the cake whispering to my soul. Its decadent richness, the delicate balance of flavors, and the enchanting hue seemed to embody pure culinary artistry. In that moment, I knew that I had stumbled upon something extraordinary—a creation that deserved to be shared with the world.

Intrigued and inspired, I resolved to unravel the secrets of this divine dessert. I dedicated myself to mastering the art of baking the perfect red velvet cake. Countless hours were spent poring over recipes, studying techniques, and experimenting in my humble kitchen. Flour dusted the air as I sieved and measured, eggs cracked with precision, and butter and sugar blended in sweet harmony.

After countless trials and a few delightful mishaps, I finally perfected my red velvet cake recipe. Each slice emerged from the oven with a moist crumb and a rich scarlet hue that mirrored the original masterpiece that had ignited my passion. But my journey had only just begun.

Armed with my newfound skills and unwavering determination, I decided to share my creation with the world. I established a small bakery, where the tantalizing aroma of freshly baked red velvet cakes would waft through the air. Word spread quickly, and soon the locals and tourists alike flocked to taste the delicacy that had captured my heart.

I poured my soul into every cake I baked, ensuring that each one carried the essence of that first bite in London. And as the cakes graced the lips of my customers, their eyes would light up with the same wonder and delight that had consumed me that fateful day.

Today, my bakery stands as a testament to that serendipitous encounter in London. The love for red velvet cake continues to bring people together, and the passion that sparked within me on that vacation has become a guiding light in my life. As I see the smiles and hear the praises of those who savor my creations, I am reminded that sometimes the smallest moments can have the most profound impact.

Red velvet cake is a popular cake made with cocoa powder, buttermilk, and vinegar to give it a unique flavor and bright red color. It's often finished with a cream cheese frosting.

## Why I Love Velvet

- Simple and classic flavor: Vanilla is a classic flavor that is widely loved for its simplicity and versatility, and it can be easily paired with other flavors.
- Versatility: Vanilla cake can be dressed up or down for different occasions and can be paired with a variety of frostings, toppings, and fillings.
- Mild taste: Vanilla cake has a mild and delicate flavor that is appealing to many people and can be enjoyed as a simple treat or a special dessert.
- Nostalgia: Vanilla cake is often associated with happy memories and comfort, making it a beloved choice for many.
- Familiarity: Vanilla is a familiar flavor that is widely used in many sweet treats and baked goods, making it a popular choice for many people.

Red velvet cake is widely liked for several reasons, including:

1.      Unique color: The reddish-brown hue of the cake is appealing and adds visual interest to any dessert table.

2.      Mild chocolate flavor: The cocoa powder provides a subtle chocolate flavor, making it a great option for those who want the taste of chocolate without being overwhelmed by it.

3.      Cream cheese frosting: The cake is often topped with a rich and creamy cream cheese frosting, which adds a tangy flavor and smooth texture to the cake.

4.      Versatility: Red velvet cake can be dressed up for special occasions or kept simple for everyday enjoyment.

5.      Nostalgia: Many people associate red velvet cake with special memories and family traditions, making it a beloved treat for many.

# MY SIGNATURE RED VELVET CAKE RECIPE BY SUGARINSTINCTCAKES

- All-purpose flour – 200g
- Cocoa Powder – 12g
- Sugar – 175g
- Unsalted butter – 90g
- Unflavoured oil (preferably sunflower oil) – 35g
- Egg – 1 large
- Salt – 1/8 tsp
- Vanilla Extract – 2 tsp
- Red Food Colour – 2 tbsp
- Buttermilk – 1 cup
- Baking Soda – 1 tsp
- Baking Powder – 1 tsp
- Vinegar – 1 tsp

## METHOD;

1. Preheat the oven to 350°F (175°C). Grease and flour two 6-inch round cake pans.

2. In a medium bowl, Add the flour and baking powder.

3. Add salt, Add cocoa powder. Sieve all dry ingredients together.

4. In a stand mixer using balloon whisk attachment or in a bowl with handheld electric mixer, cream together the butter and sugar till very light and fluffy.

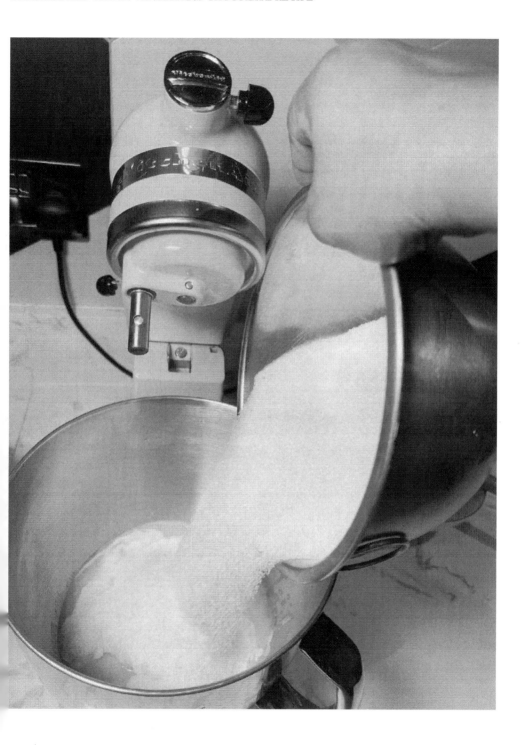

5. Slowly add oil to butter and sugar mixture and mix until well incorporated.

6. Add vanilla extract.

7. Slowly add eggs one at a time.

8. Add red food coloring or gel paste color, (I use americolor red paste, which I purchased from amazon).

9. Batter should look like this below.

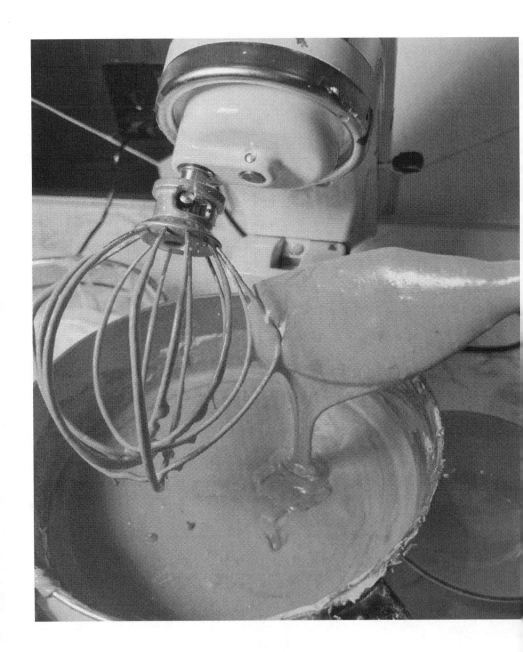

10. Switch to k-beater attachment, (it will help reduce air bubbles inside cake batter).

13. In a separate bowl. Add one cup of milk. And microwave for 1 minute or till milk is hot (You don't have to bring milk to a boil). Add 1 tablespoon to hot milk to make your one cup of buttermilk as seen in the ingredients above, and let it sit for about 5 minutes till thickened.

14. Alternate dry and wet ingredients starting with flour and alternating with buttermilk and also making sure to end with flour (DO NOT OVERMIX BATTER).

15. In a small bowl, add baking soda,

## 16. Add vinegar to baking soda,

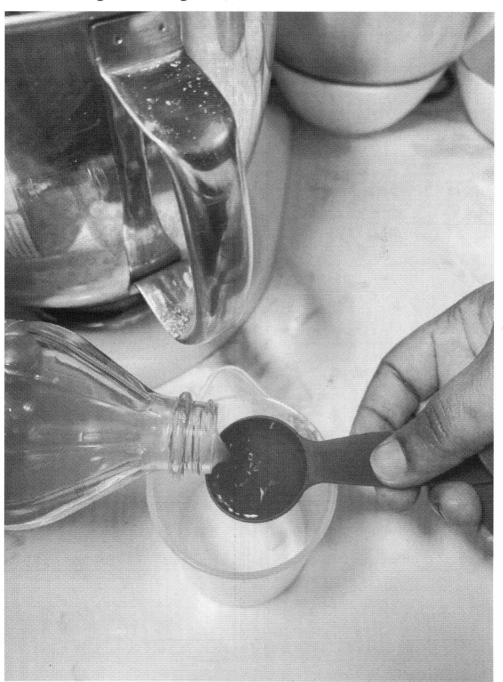

10. Mixture should bubble up and immediately fold this mixture into the batter.

11. Cake Batter should have a smooth and silky consistency and look like this.

12. Divide the batter evenly between the prepared pans. Smooth the tops with a spatula.

13. Bake for 25-30 minutes or until a toothpick inserted into the center comes out clean.

14. Remove the cakes from the oven and let them cool in the pans for 10 minutes. Then transfer to a wire rack to cool completely before frosting.

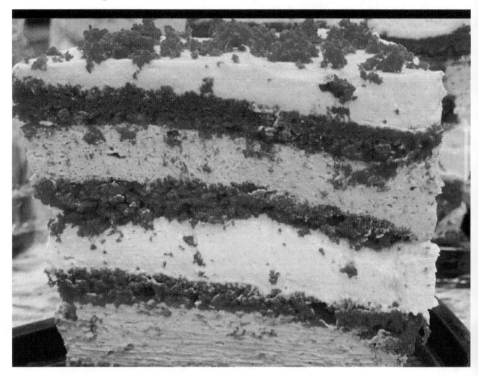

## CREAM CHEESE FROSTING

1 cup or (250ml) whipping cream ( whipping cream should be 35% fat)

¼ cup (33g) of powdered icing sugar

250g of mascarpone cream cheese

## METHOD

1.      Chill the mixing bowl, pour chilled whipping cream into the chilled bowl, then add icing sugar and vanilla extract, whip on medium until soft peaks form.

2.Take a spoon of whipped cream and add it into the mascarpone cheese, to thin the mascarpone a bit.

3.      Now add the cheese to the remaining whipped cream and whip up until stiff peaks from, it will happen quickly so keep an eye on it, its now ready for use.

OTHER RECIPES YOU CAN TRY

### 1. Red Velvet Cake with Cream Cheese Frosting

**Ingredients**:

- •      2 1/2 cups cake flour
- •      2 tablespoons unsweetened cocoa powder

- 1 teaspoon baking powder

- 1/2 teaspoon baking soda

- 1/2 teaspoon salt

- 1/2 cup unsalted butter, softened

- 1 1/2 cups granulated sugar

- 2 large eggs

- 1 cup buttermilk

- 2 teaspoons vanilla extract

- 1 tablespoon red food coloring

- 1 teaspoon distilled white vinegar

## Cream Cheese Frosting:

- 16 ounces cream cheese, softened

- 1/2 cup unsalted butter, softened

- 4 cups powdered sugar

- 1 teaspoon vanilla extract

## METHOD

1. Preheat the oven to 350°F (175°C). Grease and flour two 9-inch round cake pans.

2. In a medium bowl, sift together the cake flour, cocoa powder, baking powder, baking soda, and salt. Set aside.

3.     In a large mixing bowl, cream together the butter and sugar until light and fluffy.

4.     Beat in the eggs, one at a time, until well incorporated. Stir in the vanilla extract.

5.     In a small bowl, whisk together the buttermilk, red food coloring, and vinegar.

6.     Gradually add the dry ingredients to the batter, alternating with the buttermilk mixture. Begin and end with the dry ingredients, mixing until just combined.

7.     Divide the batter evenly between the prepared pans. Smooth the tops with a spatula.

8.     Bake for 25-30 minutes or until a toothpick inserted into the center comes out clean.

9.     Remove the cakes from the oven and let them cool in the pans for 10 minutes. Then transfer to a wire rack to cool completely.


**Cream Cheese Frosting:**

1.     In a large bowl, beat the cream cheese and butter together until smooth and creamy.

2.     Gradually add the powdered sugar and vanilla extract, beating well after each addition, until the frosting is smooth and spreadable.

3. Frost the cooled cakes, stacking them on top of each other. Decorate as desired.

## 2. Moist Red Velvet Cake with Sour Cream

**Ingredients**:

- 2 1/2 cups all-purpose flour
- 2 cups granulated sugar
- 1 tablespoon unsweetened cocoa powder
- 1 teaspoon baking soda
- 1/2 teaspoon salt
- 1 cup unsalted butter, softened
- 2 large eggs
- 1 cup buttermilk
- 1/2 cup sour cream
- 2 teaspoons vanilla extract
- 2 tablespoons red food coloring
- 1 teaspoon distilled white vinegar

## METHOD;

- Preheat the oven to 350°F (175°C). Grease and flour two 9-inch round cake pans.

- In a medium bowl, whisk together the flour, sugar, cocoa powder, baking soda, and salt. Set aside.
- In a large mixing bowl, cream together the butter and sugar until light and fluffy.
- Beat in the eggs, one at a time, until well incorporated. Stir in the vanilla extract.
- In a small bowl, combine the buttermilk, sour cream, red food coloring, and vinegar.
- Gradually add the dry ingredients to the batter, alternating with the buttermilk mixture. Begin and end with the dry ingredients, mixing until just combined.
- Divide the batter evenly between the prepared pans. Smooth the tops with a spatula.
- Bake for 25-30 minutes or until a toothpick inserted into the center comes out clean.
- Remove the cakes from the oven and let them cool in the pans for 10 minutes. Then transfer to a wire rack to cool completely before frosting.

### 3. Moist Red Velvet Cake with Pudding Mix

**Ingredients**:

- 2 1/2 cups all-purpose flour
- 1 1/2 cups granulated sugar

- 1/4 cup unsweetened cocoa powder
- 1 teaspoon baking soda
- 1/2 teaspoon salt
- 1 cup unsalted butter, softened
- 2 large eggs
- 1 cup buttermilk
- 1/2 cup sour cream
- 2 teaspoons vanilla extract
- 1/2 cup water
- 2 tablespoons red food coloring
- 1 (3.4-ounce) package instant chocolate pudding mix

## Instructions:

- Preheat the oven to 350°F (175°C). Grease and flour two 9-inch round cake pans.
- In a medium bowl, whisk together the flour, sugar, cocoa powder, baking soda, and salt. Set aside.
- In a large mixing bowl, cream together the butter and sugar until light and fluffy.
- Beat in the eggs, one at a time, until well incorporated. Stir in the vanilla extract.
- In a small bowl, combine the buttermilk, sour cream, water, red food coloring, and pudding mix.

- Gradually add the dry ingredients to the batter, alternating with the buttermilk mixture. Begin and end with the dry ingredients, mixing until just combined.
- Divide the batter evenly between the prepared pans. Smooth the tops with a spatula.
- Bake for 25-30 minutes or until a toothpick inserted into the center comes out clean.
- Remove the cakes from the oven and let them cool in the pans for 10 minutes. Then transfer to a wire rack to cool completely before frosting.

## 4. Moist Red Velvet Cake with Yogurt

**Ingredients:**

- 2 1/2 cups all-purpose flour
- 1 1/2 cups granulated sugar
- 1/4 cup unsweetened cocoa powder
- 1 teaspoon baking soda
- 1/2 teaspoon salt
- 1 cup unsalted butter, softened
- 2 large eggs
- 1 cup buttermilk
- 1/2 cup plain yogurt
- 2 teaspoons vanilla extract

- 2 tablespoons red food coloring
- 1 teaspoon distilled white vinegar

## Instructions:

- Preheat the oven to 350°F (175°C). Grease and flour two 9-inch round cake pans.
- In a medium bowl, whisk together the flour, sugar, cocoa powder, baking soda, and salt. Set aside.
- In a large mixing bowl, cream together the butter and sugar until light and fluffy.
- Beat in the eggs, one at a time, until well incorporated. Stir in the vanilla extract.
- In a small bowl, combine the buttermilk, yogurt, red food coloring, and vinegar.
- Gradually add the dry ingredients to the batter, alternating with the buttermilk mixture. Begin and end with the dry ingredients, mixing until just combined.
- Divide the batter evenly between the prepared pans. Smooth the tops with a spatula.
- Bake for 25-30 minutes or until a toothpick inserted into the center comes out clean.

- Remove the cakes from the oven and let them cool in the pans for 10 minutes. Then transfer to a wire rack to cool completely before frosting.

## 5. Moist Red Velvet Cake with Oil

## Ingredients:

- 2 1/2 cups all-purpose flour
- 2 cups granulated sugar
- 1 tablespoon unsweetened cocoa powder
- 1 teaspoon baking soda
- 1/2 teaspoon salt
- 1 cup vegetable oil
- 2 large eggs
- 1 cup buttermilk
- 2 teaspoons vanilla extract
- 1 tablespoon red food coloring
- 1 teaspoon distilled white vinegar

## Instructions:

- Preheat the oven to 350°F (175°C). Grease and flour two 9-inch round cake pans.

- In a medium bowl, whisk together the flour, sugar, cocoa powder, baking soda, and salt. Set aside.
- In a large mixing bowl, whisk together the vegetable oil, eggs, buttermilk, vanilla extract, red food coloring, and vinegar.
- Gradually add the dry ingredients to the wet ingredients, mixing until just combined.
- Divide the batter evenly between the prepared pans. Smooth the tops with a spatula.
- Bake for 25-30 minutes or until a toothpick inserted into the center comes out clean.
- Remove the cakes from the oven and let them cool in the pans for 10 minutes. Then transfer to a wire rack to cool completely before frosting.

## 6. Moist Red Velvet Cake with Beet Puree

**Ingredients:**

- 2 1/2 cups all-purpose flour
- 1 1/2 cups granulated sugar
- 2 tablespoons unsweetened cocoa powder
- 1 teaspoon baking powder
- 1/2 teaspoon baking soda
- 1/2 teaspoon salt
- 1/2 cup unsalted butter, softened

- 1/2 cup beet puree (cooked and pureed beets)
- 1 cup buttermilk
- 2 large eggs
- 2 teaspoons vanilla extract
- 1 tablespoon red food coloring

## Instructions:

- Preheat the oven to 350°F (175°C). Grease and flour two 9-inch round cake pans.
- In a medium bowl, whisk together the flour, sugar, cocoa powder, baking powder, baking soda, and salt. Set aside.
- In a large mixing bowl, cream together the butter and sugar until light and fluffy.
- Beat in the eggs, one at a time, until well incorporated. Stir in the vanilla extract.
- Add the beet puree to the batter and mix well.
- Gradually add the dry ingredients to the batter, alternating with the buttermilk. Begin and end with the dry ingredients, mixing until just combined.
- Stir in the red food coloring until evenly distributed.
- Divide the batter evenly between the prepared pans. Smooth the tops with a spatula.

- Bake for 25-30 minutes or until a toothpick inserted into the center comes out clean.
- Remove the cakes from the oven and let them cool in the pans for 10 minutes. Then transfer to a wire rack to cool completely before frosting.

Enjoy your moist red velvet cake!

# CHOCOLATE CAKE

It was a sunny morning on my 11th birthday, and anticipation swirled in the air. As I walked downstairs, I was greeted by the warm embrace of my late grandma's kitchen, filled with the comforting scent of freshly baked treats. My heart skipped a beat with excitement, for I knew something special awaited me.

And there it was, on the kitchen counter, a sight that made my eyes widen with wonder and my mouth water with anticipation: a magnificent chocolate cake, standing tall and proud. Its rich, velvety surface beckoned me closer, whispering promises of delight.

My grandma, with her kind eyes sparkling, presented the cake to me with a knowing smile. She had always been the master of the kitchen, infusing her creations with love and warmth. I could feel her love radiating from that cake, and I knew deep in my heart that this moment would forever be etched in my memory.

The first slice of cake was carefully placed on a plate, and as I took my first bite, my taste buds exploded with pure bliss. The chocolatey goodness danced upon my tongue, melting away any worries or cares that lingered. It was a moment of sheer indulgence, a celebration of life, love, and the simple joys that bring us together.

But my joy didn't end there. In a burst of excitement, I decided to share this delectable creation with my friends at school. My grandma's chocolate cake deserved to be experienced by all, and what better way to celebrate my birthday than to spread the joy among my classmates?

With my backpack slung over my shoulder and the precious cake carefully packaged, I embarked on my journey to school. The tantalizing aroma of chocolate wafted through the hallways, catching the attention of curious noses and sparking conversations among my peers.

As I entered the classroom, the anticipation in the air was palpable. I set the cake down on the table and invited my friends to gather around. Their eyes widened with excitement as they caught sight of the delectable treat before them.

One by one, I served each of my friends a generous slice of the chocolate cake, their faces lighting up with delight as they took their first bites. Joyful laughter filled the room, accompanied by murmurs of appreciation and praise for my grandma's masterpiece.

In that moment, I felt an overwhelming sense of happiness. The cake became a conduit for connection, as my friends and I shared not only a delicious treat but also a moment of pure camaraderie. The sweetness of the cake mirrored the bond we had formed, and I knew that this act of sharing had made my birthday truly special.

That day, my late grandma's chocolate cake became more than just a dessert. It became a symbol of love, cherished memories, and the power of sharing something beautiful with others. And as we laughed, ate, and reveled in the simple pleasures of life, I knew deep within my heart that my grandma's spirit was there with us, smiling upon the joy we had created together.

From that day forward, baking became a passion I would carry with me, a way to honor my grandma's legacy and to spread happiness through the art of creating delicious treats. And whenever I bake a chocolate cake, I am reminded of that magical 11th birthday, the day I discovered the power of sharing love and joy, one slice of cake at a time.

Chocolate cake is a type of cake made with cocoa powder or melted chocolate, which gives it a rich, chocolate flavor. It's a popular dessert choice for chocolate lovers and is often served with frosting, such as ganache, buttercream, or whipped cream. Chocolate cake can be made in various forms, including layer cakes, cupcakes, and sheet cakes, and can be dressed up or down for different occasions.

Chocolate cake is loved for several reasons, including:

- Flavor: The rich and indulgent taste of chocolate is widely loved and is a satisfying treat for many.
- Versatility: Chocolate cake can be dressed up or down for different occasions, from simple snacks to elaborate desserts.
- Comfort food: Chocolate cake is often associated with happy memories and comfort, making it a favorite for many people.
- Satisfying texture: The soft and tender texture of a well-made chocolate cake can be very satisfying, especially when combined with a creamy frosting.
- Universality: Chocolate is a universally loved flavor that appeals to people of all ages and cultures, making chocolate cake a popular choice for many.

## INGREDIENT NOTES

These are some of the key ingredients for this recipe, for full list of ingredients, check out the recipe below.

1.Eggs: Take them out of the fridge depending on how warm your kitchen is.

2. Whole Milk: Whole milk makes for a soft and tender cake, Measure out the whole milk and let it come to room temperature 1-2 hours before baking depending on how warm your kitchen is.

3. Oil: I recommend using a flavor neutral oil, e.g sunflower oil, canola oil, The oil makes for a super soft and tender cake.

4. Unsalted butter: Make sure your butter is 85% fat. The butter is used in the cakes, take it out of the fridge 1-2 hours before baking, you want your butter to be at room temperature.

5. All Purpose Flour: Make sure to measure it correctly. The best way to measure is by using a digital scale, if you are measuring in cups make sure the cup is well leveled, once the flour is inside the cup, you can use a knife to level the top of the measuring cup to level the flour.

6. Cocoa Powder: It is added to add a hint of cocao flavour especially in red velvet cakes.

7. Salt: It balances the sweetness and enhances the flavour of the cake.

8. Buttermilk: Its an important part of baking, it helps the leavening agent and makes the cake light and fluffy, You can use store bought or homemade method by using 1 cup of whole milk and adding 1

tablespoon of vinegar or 1 tablespoon of lemon juice , and leave at room temperature for about 10 minutes prior to use.

8. Vinegar: Its added to make the cake tender and light, it also preserves the colour when used in making red velvet cake.

# MY SIGNATURE CHOCOLATE CAKE RECIPE BY SUGARINSTINTCAKES

## INGREDIENTS

- Unsalted butter- 250g
- Sugar- 550g
- Flour- 350g
- Eggs- 4
- Baking Powder- ½ teaspoon
- Cocoa Powder- 75grams
- Boiling water- 400ml

## METHOD:

1. Preheat oven to 350F, Line the sides of your cake pan with butter and place a parchment paper on the bottom of the cake pan, set aside.

2. Add Baking Powder,

3. Baking soda,

4. Salt,

5. Add cocoa Powder,

6. Sift together the flour, baking soda, cocoa powder in a bowl and set aside.

7. Place the butter and sugar in a bowl of a stand mixer using balloon whisk attachment or hand held electric mixer. Beat on high speed until fluffy, beat on high speed until well incorporated.

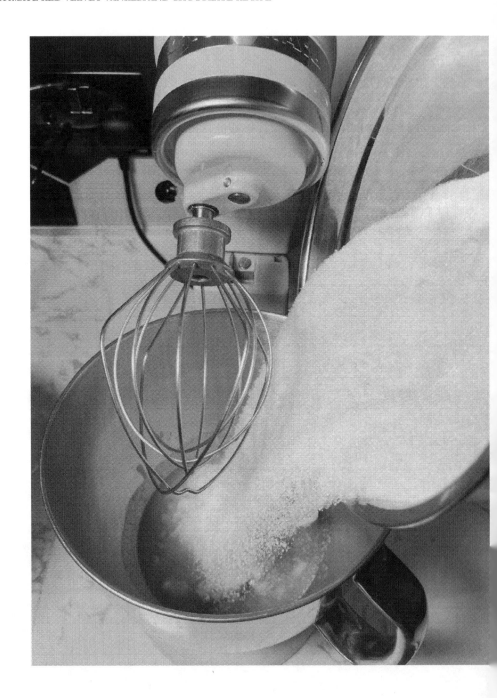

8. Add vanilla flavour,

9. Reduce speed of mixer and add the eggs one at a time, mixing slowly after each addition.

10. Cake batter should look like this.

11. Switch to a k-beater attachment and reduce mixer speed to low.

12. Reduce the mixer speed to low. Add the flour mixture in three batches slowly to the sugar, butter and egg mixture, starting with flour and also ending with flour, mix slowly and gently until almost combined,

13. Stop to scrape down the bowl as needed, cake batter should have a thick consistency like a thick paste.

14. Before the mixture is thoroughly combined, get a bowl and add the boiling hot water

15. Add in instant coffee into hot water and stir properly.

16. Slowly add hot coffee mixture into cake batter ensuring that cake batter is mixing on low speed using K-Beater. Make sure cake batter is mixed properly and has a smooth consistency.

17. Pour cake batter into a sieve to ensure a super smooth consistency.

18. Once thoroughly combined, divide your mixture into two lined 8 inches cake pans and bake accordingly for 30 minutes or until a toothpick inserted into the centre of the cake comes out clean.

19. Transfer the cake to a wire rack to cool completely.

# SUGARINSTINCTCAKES 2^ND CHOCOLATE CAKE RECIPE USING OIL

**Ingredients**:

- 2 cups all-purpose flour
- 2 cup granulated sugar
- 1 cup unsweetened cocoa powder
- 1 tsp baking powder
- 1 tsp baking soda
- 1 teaspoon of coffee
- 1 cup buttermilk
- 1 cup vegetable oil
- 2 large eggs
- 1 tsp vanilla extract
- 1 cup boiling water

**Instructions:**

1.	Preheat oven to 350°F (180°C). Grease and flour 8-inch (23cm) cake pan.

2.	In a large mixing bowl, combine flour, sugar, cocoa, baking powder, baking soda,

3.	In a separate bowl, mix buttermilk, oil, eggs, and vanilla extract.

4.	Add wet ingredients to the dry mixture and beat until well combined.

5.     Add coffee to hot water and Gradually pour in boiling water while stirring. The batter will be thin.

6.     Pour batter into the prepared pan and bake for 30-35 minutes or until a toothpick inserted into the center comes out clean.

7.     Cool the cake in the pan for 10 minutes then transfer to a wire rack to cool completely.

Enjoy your delicious chocolate cake!

# Recipe 2: Moist Chocolate Cake with Sour Cream

## Ingredients:

- 2 cups all-purpose flour
- 2 cups granulated sugar
- 3/4 cup unsweetened cocoa powder
- 1 1/2 teaspoons baking powder
- 1 1/2 teaspoons baking soda
- 1 teaspoon salt
- 1 cup sour cream
- 1/2 cup vegetable oil
- 2 large eggs
- 2 teaspoons vanilla extract
- 1 cup boiling water

## Instructions:

- Preheat the oven to 350°F (175°C). Grease and flour two 9-inch round cake pans.
- In a large mixing bowl, sift together the flour, sugar, cocoa powder, baking powder, baking soda, and salt.
- Add the sour cream, vegetable oil, eggs, and vanilla extract to the dry ingredients. Mix until well combined.

- Stir in the boiling water, a little at a time, until the batter is smooth.
- Divide the batter evenly between the prepared pans. Smooth the tops with a spatula.
- Bake for 30-35 minutes or until a toothpick inserted into the center comes out clean.
- Remove the cakes from the oven and let them cool in the pans for 10 minutes. Then transfer to a wire rack to cool completely before frosting.

Other Chocolate Recipes You Can Try:

## 1. Chocolate Lava Cake

**Ingredients:**

- 4 ounces semisweet chocolate, chopped
- 1/2 cup unsalted butter
- 1 cup powdered sugar
- 2 large eggs
- 2 large egg yolks
- 1/2 teaspoon vanilla extract
- 1/4 cup all-purpose flour
- Pinch of salt

## Instructions:

- Preheat the oven to 425°F (220°C). Grease and lightly flour four 6-ounce ramekins.

- In a microwave-safe bowl, melt the semisweet chocolate and butter together, stirring occasionally until smooth. Let it cool slightly.

- In a mixing bowl, whisk together the powdered sugar, eggs, egg yolks, and vanilla extract.

- Pour the melted chocolate mixture into the egg mixture and whisk until well combined.

- Stir in the flour and salt until just combined.

- Divide the batter evenly among the prepared ramekins.

- Place the ramekins on a baking sheet and bake for 12-14 minutes or until the edges are set but the centers are still soft.

- Remove the cakes from the oven and let them cool for 1 minute.

- Carefully invert each ramekin onto a serving plate and gently lift to remove. The cakes should release easily.

- Serve immediately with a dusting of powdered sugar, a scoop of ice cream, or a dollop of whipped cream.

## 2. Chocolate Raspberry Cake

## Ingredients:

- For the cake:
- 1 3/4 cups all-purpose flour
- 1 1/2 cups granulated sugar
- 3/4 cup unsweetened cocoa powder
- 1 1/2 teaspoons baking powder
- 1 1/2 teaspoons baking soda
- 1 teaspoon salt
- 2 large eggs
- 1 cup milk
- 1/2 cup vegetable oil
- 2 teaspoons vanilla extract
- 1 cup boiling water

## For the raspberry filling:

- 2 cups fresh raspberries
- 1/4 cup granulated sugar
- 1 tablespoon cornstarch

## For the chocolate ganache:

- 8 ounces semisweet chocolate, chopped
- 1 cup heavy cream.

## Instructions:

- Preheat the oven to 350°F (175°C). Grease and flour two 9-inch round cake pans.
- In a large mixing bowl, sift together the flour, sugar, cocoa powder, baking powder, baking soda, and salt.
- Add the eggs, milk, vegetable oil, and vanilla extract to the dry ingredients. Mix until well combined.
- Gradually pour in the boiling water, stirring continuously, until the batter is smooth.
- Pour the batter into the prepared cake pans and smooth the tops with a spatula.
- Bake for 30-35 minutes or until a toothpick inserted into the center comes out clean.
- Remove the cakes from the oven and let them cool in the pans for 10 minutes. Then transfer to a wire rack to cool completely.
- In a saucepan, combine the raspberries, sugar, and cornstarch. Cook over medium heat, stirring constantly, until the mixture thickens. Remove from heat and let it cool completely.
- Place one cake layer on a serving plate. Spread the raspberry filling evenly over the top.
- Place the second cake layer on top of the filling.

- In a saucepan, heat the heavy cream until it begins to simmer. Remove from heat and pour over the chopped semisweet chocolate. Stir until smooth and glossy.
- Pour the ganache over the top of the cake, allowing it to drip down the sides.
- Refrigerate the cake for at least 1 hour to allow the ganache to set.
- Serve and enjoy!

### 3. Flourless Chocolate Cake

**Ingredients:**

- 1 cup unsalted butter
- 8 ounces semisweet chocolate, chopped
- 1 1/2 cups granulated sugar
- 6 large eggs
- 1 cup unsweetened cocoa powder
- 1 teaspoon vanilla extract
- 1/4 teaspoon salt

**Instructions:**

o Preheat the oven to 325°F (165°C). Grease a 9-inch round cake pan and line the bottom with parchment paper.

o In a microwave-safe bowl, melt the butter and chopped chocolate together, stirring occasionally until smooth. Let it cool slightly.

o In a large mixing bowl, whisk together the sugar, eggs, cocoa powder, vanilla extract, and salt.

o Pour the melted chocolate mixture into the egg mixture and whisk until well combined.

o Pour the batter into the prepared cake pan and smooth the top with a spatula.

o Bake for 35-40 minutes or until a toothpick inserted into the center comes out with a few moist crumbs.

o Remove the cake from the oven and let it cool in the pan for 10 minutes. Then transfer to a wire rack to cool completely before serving.

## 4. Vegan Chocolate Cake

**Ingredients:**

o 2 cups all-purpose flour

o 1 1/2 cups granulated sugar

o 1/2 cup unsweetened cocoa powder

o 2 teaspoons baking powder

o 1 1/2 teaspoons baking soda

o 1/2 teaspoon salt

o 1 3/4 cups almond milk (or any non-dairy milk)

o 1/2 cup vegetable oil

o 2 tablespoons apple cider vinegar

o 2 teaspoons vanilla extract

**Instructions:**

o Preheat the oven to 350°F (175°C). Grease and flour two 9-inch round cake pans.

o In a large mixing bowl, whisk together the flour, sugar, cocoa powder, baking powder, baking soda, and salt.

o In a separate bowl, whisk together the almond milk, vegetable oil, apple cider vinegar, and vanilla extract.

o Pour the wet ingredients into the dry ingredients and mix until well combined.

o Divide the batter evenly between the prepared pans. Smooth the tops with a spatula.

o Bake for 30-35 minutes or until a toothpick inserted into the center comes out clean.

o Remove the cakes from the oven and let them cool in the pans for 10 minutes. Then transfer to a wire rack to cool completely before frosting.

## 5. Chocolate Fudge Cake

**Ingredients:**

o 2 cups all-purpose flour

o 2 cups granulated sugar

o 3/4 cup unsweetened cocoa powder

o 2 teaspoons baking powder

o 1 1/2 teaspoons baking soda

o 1 teaspoon salt

o 1 cup milk

o 1/2 cup vegetable oil

o 2 large eggs

o 2 teaspoons vanilla extract

o 1 cup boiling water

- o 1/2 cup unsalted butter
- o 2/3 cup evaporated milk
- o 1 2/3 cups granulated sugar
- o 2 cups semisweet chocolate chips
- o 1 teaspoon vanilla extract

## Instructions:

- Preheat the oven to 350°F (175°C). Grease and flour two 9-inch round cake pans.
- In a large mixing bowl, sift together the flour, sugar, cocoa powder, baking powder, baking soda, and salt.
- Add the milk, vegetable oil, eggs, and vanilla extract to the dry ingredients. Mix until well combined.
- Stir in the boiling water, a little at a time, until the batter is smooth.
- Divide the batter evenly between the prepared pans. Smooth the tops with a spatula.
- Bake for 30-35 minutes or until a toothpick inserted into the center comes out clean.
- Remove the cakes from the oven and let them cool in the pans for 10 minutes. Then transfer to a wire rack to cool completely before frosting.

- In a saucepan, combine the butter, evaporated milk, and granulated sugar. Cook over medium heat, stirring constantly, until the mixture comes to a boil.

- Remove the saucepan from the heat and stir in the chocolate chips and vanilla extract. Continue stirring until the chocolate chips are melted and the frosting is smooth.

- Let the frosting cool for a few minutes, then spread it over the cooled cakes. Enjoy!

# FAQ (Frequently Asked Questions)

**1. What is the purpose of eggs in baking?**

- Eggs provide structure, moisture, and richness in baked goods.

**2. How can I make my cakes fluffy?**

- Make sure the eggs are at room temperature, beat butter and sugar together until light and fluffy, and make sure to sift the flour..

**1. Why do my cakes falling or sinking in the middle?**

- It can be due to overmixing the batter, using too much flour, or not using enough leavening agents. : There are a few possible reasons for cakes sinking in the middle. Firstly, make sure not to overmix the batter, as this can create too much air, causing the cake to collapse. Additionally, check that your oven temperature is accurate and stable throughout baking. Opening the oven door too frequently can also cause fluctuations in temperature. Finally, ensure that the cake is fully baked before removing it from the oven by using a toothpick or cake tester to check for doneness

### 2. Can I use baking powder instead of baking soda?

No, they are not interchangeable and serve different purposes in baking.

### 3. Can I freeze my cakes?

YES, Unfrosted cakes can be frozen for up to 2 months, cool completely before wrapping in plastic wrap and then foil and freeze in an airtight container, thaw to room temperature and start adding the cream cheese frosting.

### 4. How do I properly cream butter and sugar for cake baking?

A: To cream butter and sugar for cake baking, start with softened butter at room temperature. Place the butter in a mixing bowl and beat it with an electric mixer on medium speed until creamy. Gradually add the sugar, a little at a time, while continuing to beat the mixture. Beat the butter and sugar together until light and fluffy, which usually takes 3-5 minutes. Scrape down the sides of the bowl occasionally to ensure even mixing..

**5. How do I make my cake layers level and flat?**

**A:** To make your cake layers level and flat, you can use a long serrated knife or a cake leveler. Once the cakes have cooled, place them on a flat surface and carefully slice off any domed or uneven portions of the cake. You can also invest in cake baking strips or use a moist towel wrapped around the cake pans during baking to help promote even baking and prevent excessive doming.

**6. How can I make a cake moist and tender?**

**A:** To make a cake moist and tender, you can incorporate ingredients such as buttermilk, yogurt, sour cream, or vegetable oil into the batter. These ingredients add moisture and fat, resulting in a tender texture. Additionally, avoid overbaking the cake, as it can lead to dryness. Follow the recommended baking time and test the cake's doneness by inserting a toothpick into the center. If it comes out with a few moist crumbs, the cake is done.

**7. How do I prevent my cake from sticking to the pan?**

A: To prevent your cake from sticking to the pan, make sure to properly grease and flour the pan. Use melted butter, vegetable oil, or cooking spray to grease the pan, ensuring you coat all surfaces. Dust the greased pan with flour, tapping out any excess. You can also use parchment paper or wax paper to line the bottom of the pan, which makes it easier to remove the cake after baking.

**8. How do I know when a cake is fully baked?**

**A:** The best way to determine if a cake is fully baked is by using a toothpick or cake tester. Insert it into the center of the cake, and if it comes out clean or with a few moist crumbs, the cake is done. Another method is gently pressing the center of the cake with your fingertip; if it springs back lightly and doesn't leave an indentation, it is likely fully baked. Remember to follow the recommended baking time as a guideline and avoid opening the oven too frequently while the cake is baking.

These are some of the most frequently asked questions when it comes to baking cakes. I hope these answers are helpful to you!

# MY MESSAGE TO YOU

In a world filled with flavors and scents, my heart has always been captivated by the magical realm of baking. The mere thought of creating exquisite cakes, each layer oozing with the richness of Red Velvet, Vanilla, and Chocolate, has been my driving force. As a budding baker, I embarked on a journey that was as delicate as folding egg whites into batter, as challenging as getting the perfect crumb, and as rewarding as watching smiles spread across the faces of those who indulged in my creations.

Chapter 1: The First Rise

My journey began with a simple vanilla cupcake. Fueled by enthusiasm and armed with my newfound passion, I threw myself into the art of baking. But as every baker knows, perfection doesn't come overnight. My initial attempts were far from the heavenly delicacies I aspired to create. Countless batches crumbled, leaving me questioning my abilities. Doubt clouded my thoughts, and I found myself questioning if I was cut out to be a baker.

Chapter 2: The Bitter Chocolate Truth

In the face of adversity, I discovered that failure was not a dead-end but a stepping stone towards mastery. I embraced each mistake as an opportunity to learn. With determination, I decided to conquer the enigmatic world of chocolate. From tempering to ganache, I immersed myself in its complexities. Sometimes, it felt like battling a temperamental molten beast, but I never backed down. The chocolaty journey taught me the importance of patience and dedication, as every cacao-drenched success was worth the struggle.

Chapter 3: The Red Velvet Revelation

Just when my confidence was soaring high with my chocolate conquest, the allure of Red Velvet seduced me with its crimson charm. But this alluring delight came with its unique set of challenges. The elusive moistness, the perfect balance of tangy and sweet – it all seemed like an impossible dream. However, I was committed to unraveling its mysteries. Through trial and error, I learned the subtle art of creating the quintessential Red Velvet. My kitchen turned into a laboratory of passion, as I experimented with various techniques and ingredients. And finally, I succeeded, unlocking the secrets to the ultimate Red Velvet cake.

Chapter 4: Rising to New Heights

With Vanilla, Chocolate, and Red Velvet under my belt, I stood tall as a baker, but the journey was far from over. Each day, I embraced fresh inspirations, continuously expanding my repertoire. But amidst the successes, there were days when exhaustion tried to crumble my resolve. Doubts crept back in, and I questioned if my efforts were worthwhile. In those moments, I remembered my humble beginnings and the fervent desire that ignited my love for baking. It was a passion that transcended the trials and fueled my perseverance.

Conclusion: The Joy of Never Giving Up

To all aspiring bakers out there, let my journey be a testament that with unwavering passion and an unyielding spirit, you can overcome any challenge. Embrace every failure as an opportunity to grow and learn. Stay humble in your triumphs, for there is always something new to discover. Surround yourself with fellow bakers who understand your journey and can offer support in times of doubt.

Remember, the joy of baking lies not just in the final product, but in the process itself. With every whisk of the batter, every sprinkle of sugar, and every blissful aroma filling the air, you'll find a fulfillment that makes the struggles worthwhile. Embrace the sweetness of the journey, and let it fuel your motivation to never give up on your dreams.

So, let your ovens be your canvas, and your heart be the chef. Go forth, dear bakers, and create the most delightful symphony of flavors the world has ever tasted. Your sweet journey awaits!

Made in the USA
Monee, IL
06 December 2024

f22ecf3c-69b5-4dc6-a579-73a5feaa6972R01